Camila and Clay~Old~Woman

Mary Cappellini with Tito Naranjo
Illustrated by Shonto Begay

Rigby

To Tito Naranjo and his talented family of Santa Clara Pueblo in
New Mexico. I was inspired by their writings, poems, books,
and pottery—and especially by my conversations with Tito.
—M.C.

ACKNOWLEDGMENTS

Thanks to Christina Tostado of the Bowers Museum in
Santa Ana, California, who introduced me to Pueblo Pottery.
Special thanks to Bently Spang, an American Indian
artist who introduced me to the Naranjo family.

© 1997 by Rigby,
a division of Reed Elsevier, Inc.
500 Coventry Lane
Crystal Lake, IL 60014

All rights reserved. No part of this publication
may be reproduced or transmitted in any form
or by any means, electronic or mechanical,
including photocopying, recording, taping, or
any information storage and retrieval system,
without permission in writing from the publisher.

00 99 98 97 96
10 9 8 7 6 5 4 3 2 1

Printed in the United States of America

ISBN 0-7635-3137-5

Camila woke up early and knew it was a special day. It was the day she would be going to her grandmother Gia Rosa's house to make pottery. This made her very happy.

Camila knew that she would learn a lot about the traditions of her family and her Tewa ancestors. Camila smiled. She was pleased to know that her cousins and her aunts—and, of course, her mother—would be there, too. Camila knew that getting together like this always made her feel like she was part of a much larger family.

4

When Camila arrived with her mother at the plaza in Santa Clara Pueblo, she could see Gia Rosa's house. Gia Rosa was working as she waited outside to greet all her children and grandchildren. They could see that she was very happy, too.

While she waited for her cousins, Camila saw Pueblo people beginning their daily work. She also saw tourists arriving at the plaza. They came early to this small Tewa pueblo in northern New Mexico to buy its famous pottery.

Camila thought she might even see her Aunt Cecilia selling something to tourists in the plaza. Camila dreamed that one day she would be able to make pottery like her Aunt Cecilia and sell it in the plaza, too.

Little by little, Camila's cousins and aunts arrived. Gia Rosa had coffee and blue cornmeal bread waiting for them. They talked and ate.

Then they gathered around a large table covered with clay. They started to form jars, pots, and figures out of the clay. Camila liked to feel the clay between her fingers. While she touched it, she thought of Clay-Old-Woman. Gia Rosa had told her that Clay-Old-Woman was a spirit that lived in the earth and clay. Gia Rosa had also told Camila to respect Clay-Old-Woman and to listen to her breathe inside the shapes as Camila was making them. The spirit would live on in these new creations.

Camila worked next to Gia Rosa. Her pottery always turned out better when she was at her grandmother's side. Camila felt Clay-Old-Woman in her hands while she worked. Everyone talked and laughed, but Camila was quiet. She was listening to the spirit.

"Look what I made," said her cousin Felipe as he showed them all a lizard. Cousin Tony made little animals that he also shared with pride. Gina and Lupe were laughing while they worked together on a large figure. Aunt Clara was making a water jar. Gia Rosa and Camila's mother, Maria, were making large bowls.

Camila watched Aunt Cecilia finish a large pot. Her aunt was pinching and scraping the coils of clay to create a smooth surface. She was a famous potter. Aunt Cecilia had won many awards at the Indian Market.

Camila would love to win an award one day, but she would always remember what Gia Rosa said. "It is much more important to learn how to work with and respect the clay than to win awards."

Camila wasn't so sure. She knew that Aunt Cecilia earned a lot of money. Her aunt made more money by selling one pot than her parents did in an entire month. However, Camila knew that her mother would not sell her pots to tourists. She said that each pot was a piece of Clay-Old-Woman and should not be sold. Her mother would rather give away her pots to friends to express her feelings.

I don't know, thought Camila. *Sometimes I wish my mother would sell her pottery instead of working at the store. She would earn more money, and she could stay at home with me.*

Camila was looking at her cousins' new clothes and new shoes. She wished she could have new things, too. Her mother always told her not to compare herself to others or to desire other people's things, but that was difficult for Camila.

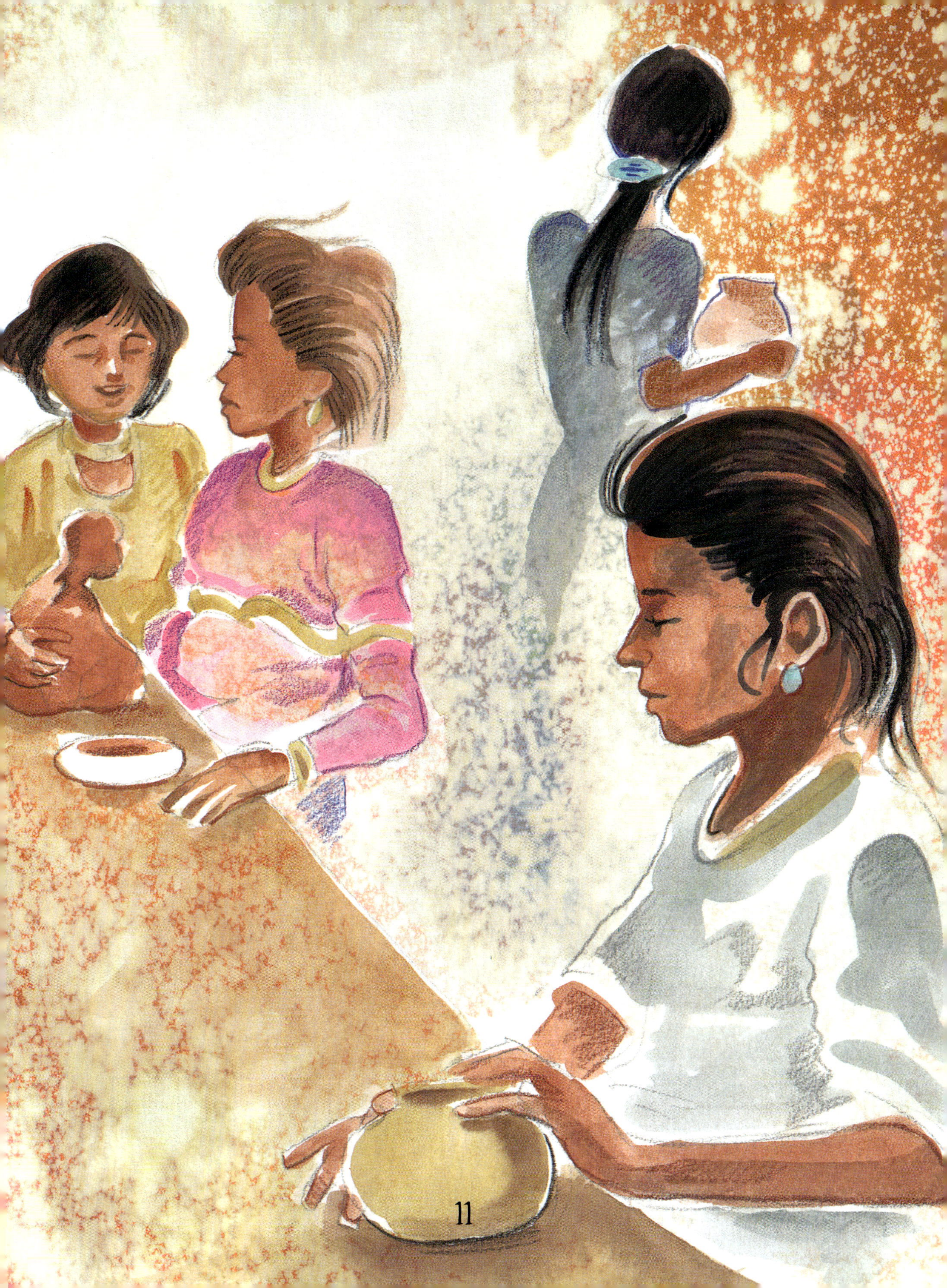

"Have you finished, my child?" asked her mother. Camila looked at her small pot. She was not very pleased with what she had created.

"I think Clay-Old-Woman is not helping me today," said Camila. She thought that maybe her desires were bothering Clay-Old-Woman.

Gia Rosa looked at Camila's pot and said, "I think it has a good shape. Your pot will be very pretty when it is finished." Camila felt a little better with these kind words from her grandmother.

After working all morning, they put their wet pottery in a safe place to dry. They knew that the pottery might break if it was touched while drying.

"Who wants to drive to the mountains with me tomorrow to dig up more clay?" asked Gia Rosa.

Camila really wanted to go, but her mother said that they couldn't go.

Camila was disappointed. She had learned from her grandmother that gathering and preparing the clay by hand was the traditional way. Her people had been doing it this way for many years and would continue doing it for years to come. The adults would always teach their children.

The following week Camila and the rest of her family returned to Gia Rosa's house. "I can't wait to see how our pottery turns out!" said Gia Rosa when everyone had arrived.

First they began to sand the pieces with sandpaper. Camila sat down between her grandmother and her mother, and she watched them sand their large bowls. They were sanding the bowls in small circles. Camila worked hard at making her pot as smooth as possible, sanding it like her mother and grandmother were doing. They, in turn, noticed that Camila was learning this step in the pottery-making process very well.

"I think you're doing a fine job sanding your pot, Camila," said her grandmother.

When they had all finished sanding, the adults took out small, hard, smooth stones for the important step of polishing their pieces. Most of the stones had been in their family for a very long time.

Gia Rosa said, "Come with me, Camila. I have something special for you."

15

Gia Rosa took Camila to another room and pulled open a drawer in a cabinet. She reached into the drawer and pulled out a very special stone.

"This is a polishing stone that my grandmother gave to me when I was a little girl. Now I am giving it to you." She put the stone in Camila's hand.

Camila accepted the stone with pride. She knew that she was continuing an important tradition. She returned to the table and sat down to polish her pot with the special stone her grandmother had given her.

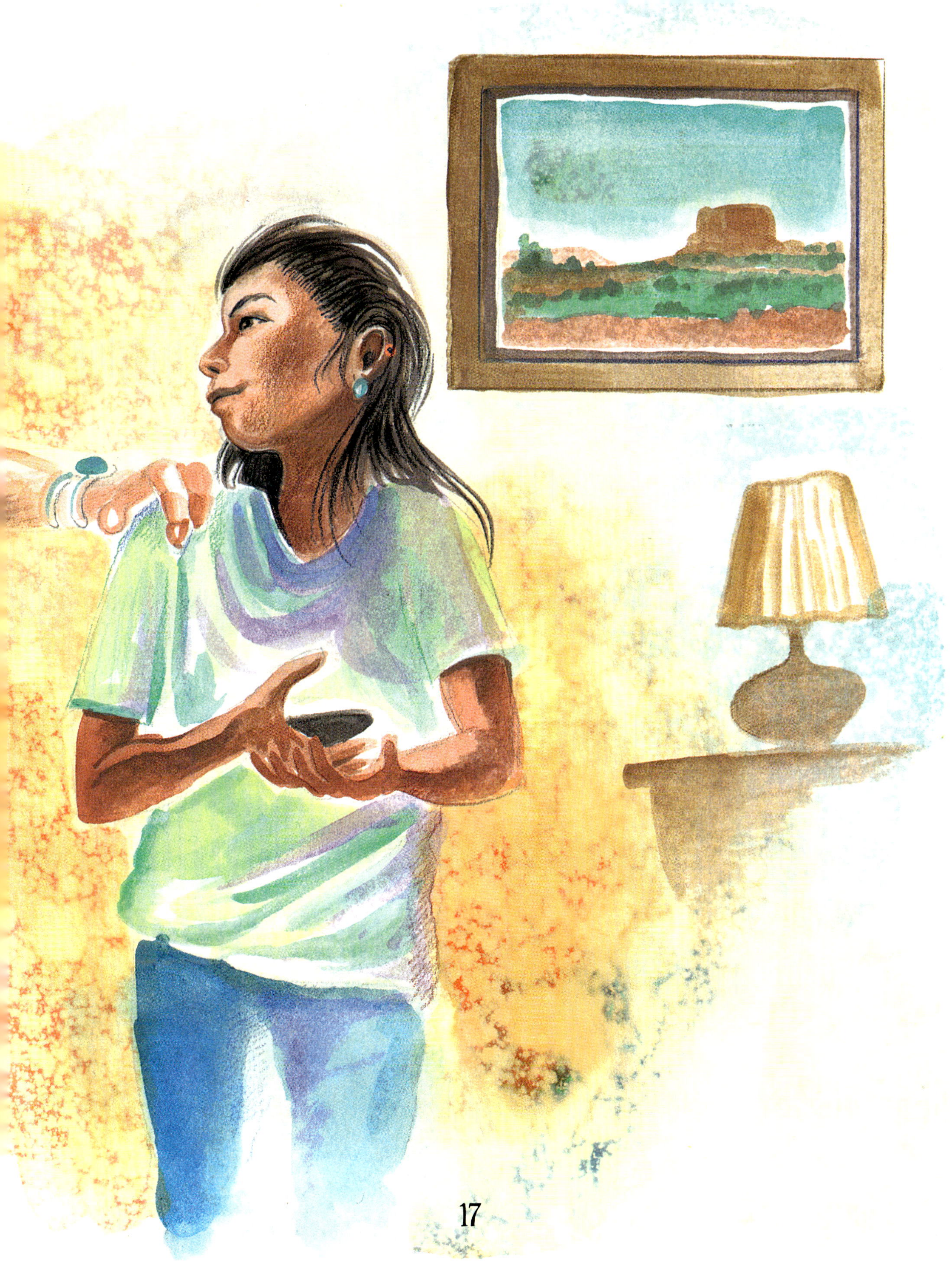

When Camila finished polishing, she wanted to do something very special and original to decorate her pot. She could feel that Clay-Old-Woman was with her today. With her help, Camila knew that she could create something unique.

She thought about the traditional designs of Santa Clara Pueblo, like the water serpent and the bear paw, but she wanted to paint animals that she saw every day. So she decided to paint a fish in the river and a cat at the water's edge, eyeing it with desire.

She used a fine, wet clay called slip to paint her pot. First she used a red base slip. Then she used black and white slips to paint the design.

"How original!" said Gia Rosa.

"Look at how well she can paint!" said Aunt Cecilia. "I want to enter her pot in the Indian Market. I think she can win in the children's show."

Camila was surprised at the attention. She was happy, thinking about the possibility of winning an award like her Aunt Cecilia had won. Then her mother said, "Let's see what happens to the pot when we put it in the fire." She was reminding Camila that it could break.

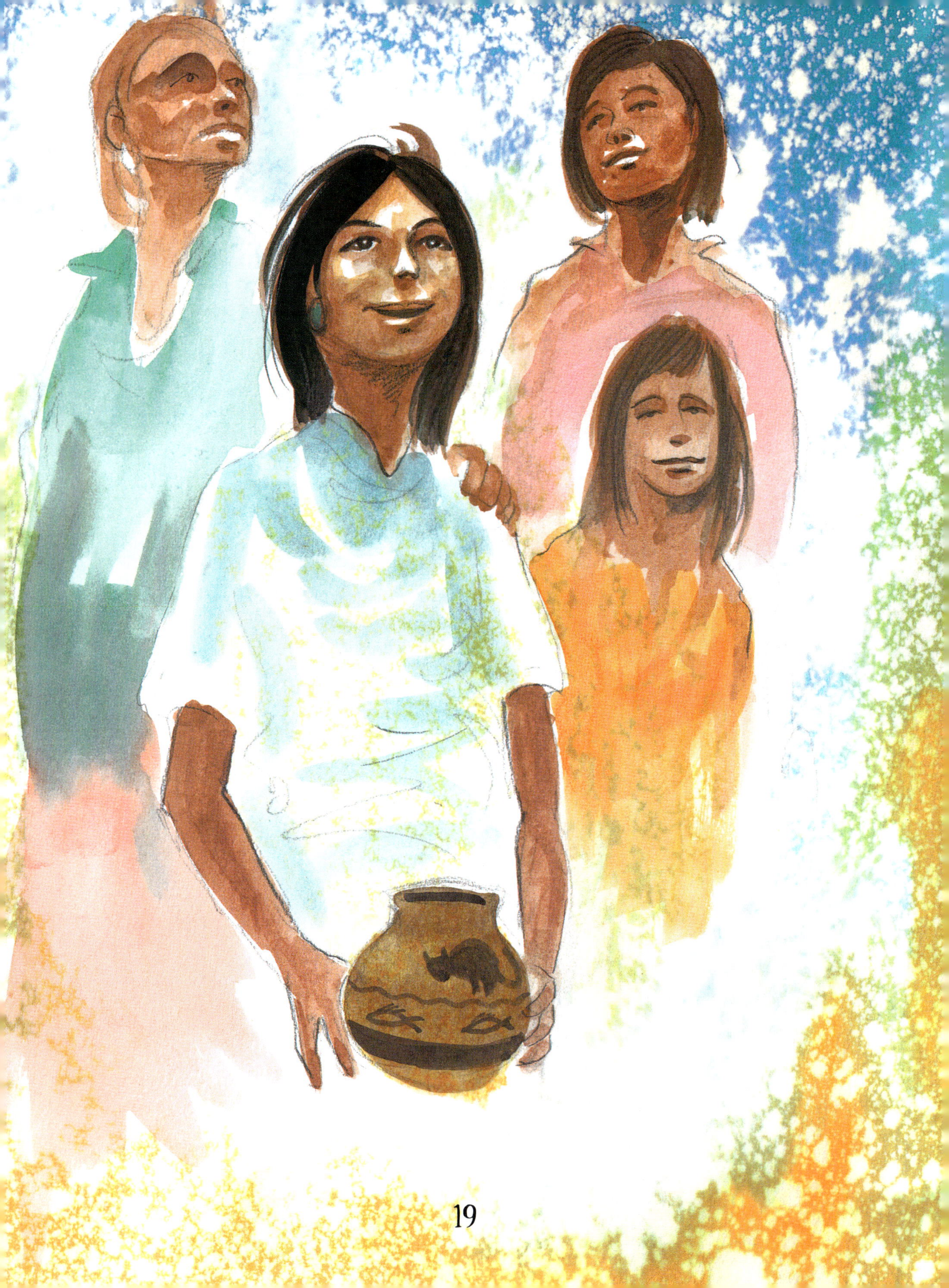

Camila waited nervously for the day of the firing. All of the family met outside Aunt Cecilia's house to make the fire. They helped gather wood, and they put the pieces of clay on a metal rack. Gia Rosa covered the clay pieces with a metal top so the flames wouldn't touch the pieces directly. Camila asked Clay-Old-Woman to watch over her pot in the fire.

While the fire was burning, Camila was very nervous. If she heard a loud noise, it would mean that a pot had broken or exploded in the fire. She waited, but heard nothing.

When the fire finally died down, Camila could see her pot. It was perfect, and the firing made the painted figures stand out even better than before!

Aunt Cecilia was the first to congratulate her niece. She said that she would enter Camila's pot in the children's show at the Indian Market. Camila knew her mother did not like the idea but would still allow her to enter.

Gia Rosa said to Camila, "My child, never forget that the clay does not belong to you. It has life. Clay-Old-Woman lends us the clay to use it wisely. When you work with it, you are connected to the spirits of the past. You have a talent that was given to you. You should use it well."

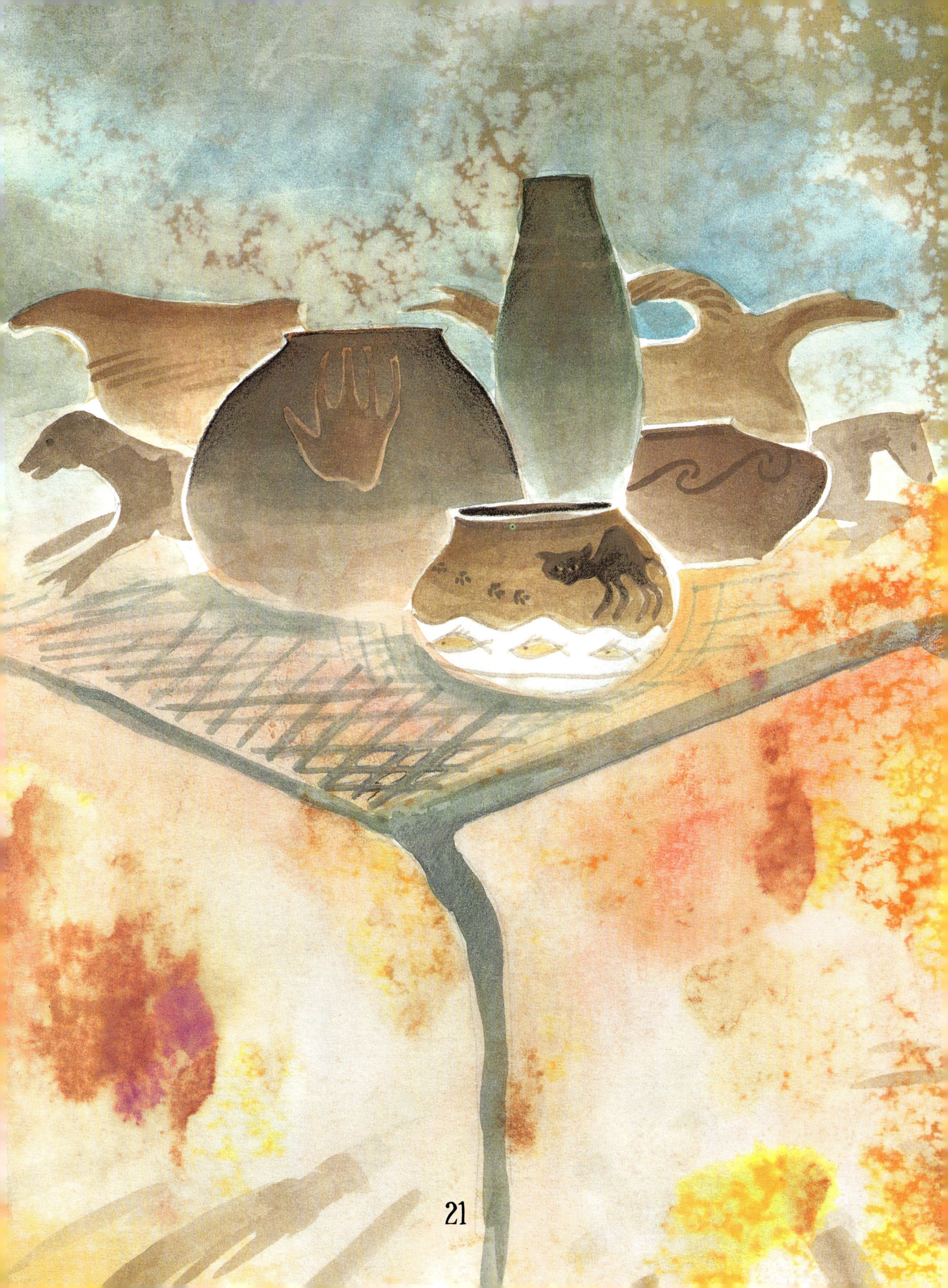

Camila went with her Aunt Cecilia to the Indian Market the following week. She had never been there before. She couldn't believe how many pots were in the show. How could the judges decide which pot was the best? All the pots looked so good. Camila realized that there were many talented children. She thought it would be difficult to win.

She spent hours looking at all of the pieces to be in the show and at all the people buying and selling pots. She felt confused and upset. Maybe her mother was right when she had asked, "How can you sell a piece of Clay-Old-Woman?" She wasn't sure she wanted to be a part of this.

Although her aunt was very busy selling pottery, Camila asked Aunt Cecilia to take her home. She was very tired. Her aunt dropped her off and returned to the Indian Market to continue selling pots. Camila went to her room, feeling sad and tired.

The next day Camila and her mother were making dinner in the kitchen. Aunt Cecilia came to the door with a great big smile on her face. "Camila, Camila!" she shouted, "You won!"

Camila couldn't believe it. She was so surprised. "Mom, I won!" she yelled. "I won an award like Aunt Cecilia!"

Her mother looked at her and said, "That's wonderful, Camila. The judges could see that you have talent. Now you can decide what to do with your gift."

Camila thought for a moment. "Mom, thanks to you and Gia Rosa, I have learned the true value of my talent. I hope Clay-Old-Woman will always want to live inside my creations."